I, teacher

Sophie Higson

Presentation by *BookLeaf Publishing*

Web: www.bookleafpub.com

E-mail: info@bookleafpub.com

ISBN: 9789357690232

First edition 2022

For Hector, who inspired this book.

PREFACE

Writing 21 poems written in 21 days, was inspired by recent events at my school. I found that expressing my feelings using pen and paper was helpful. I would recommend poetry to everyone, as a way to say what you want to when you can't find the words out loud.

September Sonnet

Oh Summer, have you really gone away?
The weeks were long, those evenings light and free.
Once more we set alarm clocks to obey,
the ironing board resumes its dull decree.
My flip-flopped feet are pinched by hardened shoes,
and tailored trousers cram in August's gain.
My car rejoins relentless rush-hour queues,
as I brace myself to operate my brain.
The seating plans are printed on the desk,
my timetable and planner are in hand.
Yet any apprehension I possess
diffuses as in front of you I stand.
Your too-big blazers, fresh to start the term.
Your bright-eyed eager faces wait to learn.

Year 8

Some people love to hate
Year 8.

Most of them are great

Of course they aggravate
at times

But so can Year 9s.

Privilege

I may sow the seed
but then I watch you grow,

I may unlock the door
but you must enter on your own.

I may support and guide you
but never tell you who to be.

I may show you where to look
but don't tell you what to see.

I may spark the light
but yours is the flame that burns.

I may be the teacher
but I'm the one who learns.

Balance

It's hard to get the balance right
get up at dawn
or work at night.

No matter how much time you spend
that pile of work
will never end.

So learn to stop and put it down
and set your feet
back on the ground.

For the most important work of all
is that within
your own four walls.

Passwords

328 passwords
to unlock the places I need
to remember
or
reset
No, I am not a robot.
But sometimes I wish I was.

Duty

You might have time to go to the loo
and time to grab a cup of tea too.
before turning up on time, as you must.

And time really crawls
as you walk around the hall,
or patrol up and down
the busy playground.

(You have probably got a million other things
you could be doing)
But this is another kind of work.
So as those slow minutes turn,
use them to learn.

Use them to watch and see,
how children are when they are free.
Watch the quiet girl from class as she squeals
with her friends,

Notice who they really are and how they choose
to spend
their time.
See who is sitting on their own.

It's important you don't moan about the time.

It might be the most important time
of your day.

Parents evening

Five minutes
to summarise
someone's most important
Someone.

Ode to the Snow day

As darkness descends upon a winter's night
and flakes are softly falling on the lawn,
whispers of the forecast bring delight
and prayers that it continues until dawn.

All eyes observe the ever falling snow
as inch by glorious inch it coats the ground,
tomorrow in the morning we might know-
cascading from above that happy sound;

 "Snow day! School is closed! A snow day!"
(they might say)
"Put down your pens, wrap up and go outdoors."
But all our hope could turn into dismay,
If when we wake, the white world is no more.

Email

The tide comes in,
every morning.
Look out, as
they roll in
to outlook.
Waves flood the filling inbox
submerging the bottomless deep with new
requests.
Ever rolling wave
after wave
after wave
As the waves break but
there is no break
Emails buried under
Emails buried
under emails
buried.

One has a flag,
waving wildly in the hope it might be seen.

Staff room

I don't know your shoe size
or the lies you've told
your favourite scent, your deepest fears
or views on growing old.

I don't know how you take your tea or
what keeps you up at night,
the car you drive, your greatest love,
or if you'd win a fight.

It's safe to say I might not
even know your name...

but in here, these things don't matter
you're in my corner, we are the same.

Don't count the days

Twelve teachers crying
Eleven hours of marking
Ten bells a ringing
Nine boys are chancing
Eight made up meetings
Seven souls are sinking
Six hairs are greying
Five cold teas
Four falling grades
Three felt pens
Two weeks off
And a sore throat just for me.
(Zero snow days)

Inset Haiku

You can wake up late
and wear jeans if you want to
Then, crash! Into the new term.

Lament

You were on my

to-do
list, and now

I don't know what
to do

with your empty chair
since you're not there.

Remote learning (part 1)

The cat sat on the mat
The cat sat on my lap
The cat sat on my laptop.

Quality assurance

Some days I am outstanding
Some days I am quite good
and some days
I require improvement.

Most days I am a bit of all three.

But everyday
I am here, trying.

Mock exam

There once was a poor Year 11
who'd coasted along since Year 7
he had a big shock
after sitting his mock.
Next time he might do some revision.

Test

Empty papers handed out
in the hope they'll soon be full
of all the many things
I've taught you

(don't forget to write your name)

Pens are ready, steady, go
What do they know?
What will it show?

(and don't forget to write your name)

Some are bursting with words,
keenly scribbling.
Others, just stare for ages
at blank pages
thinking-
am I good enough?

And I'm thinking, am I good enough?

(you didn't write your name)
But there's always one.

Remote learning (part 2)

Your faces are all squares
Is everybody there?
You brother might be cute
But can you please press mute.
I'm going to share my screen,
talking to a machine.
I know we are all reaching
Can you call this teaching?
The silence is concerning
Are you even learning?
There's slippers on my feet
And clapping on the street.

Genius

Sometimes you meet a student who
has clearly got more brains than you

and so you need to find a way
to ensure you don't betray

your lack of brain.

Our job as teachers isn't to
be cleverer than all of you.

We plan, we coach, we motivate
with passion as our greatest trait.

Usain Bolt might win the race
his coach would not have half his pace.

Fire drill

It all depends
when it happens.

It could be during PSHE
when teaching year 8 puberty.

It could be in a topic test
and students now won't do their best.

But the worst time, which is just no good
Is when you've got a free period.

Lesson observation prayer

God grant me the serenity
to plan and teach a well structured lesson,
that promotes a love of learning and engages
my pupils' intellectual curiosity.
Whilst at the same time promotes good progress
(as I am accountable for attainment)
and can stretch and challenge everyone.
Also grant me courage to make accurate use of
formative and summative assessment,
and the wisdom to know the difference.
May my lesson be well structured,
demonstrate good subject knowledge,
and be adapted for all pupils,
(of both high ability and with additional needs.)
Pray that I will manage behaviour effectively,
using praise and sanctions consistently and fairly,
trusting that the boy sitting at the back,
will make all things right, and surrender to my will.
That I may be reasonably happy with my lesson plan,
and supremely happy with him.

Amen